Charming Mandala Coloring

Copyright: Published in the United States by Ivana Pisano
Published December 2016
ISBN-13: 978-1541253018
ISBN-10: 1541253019

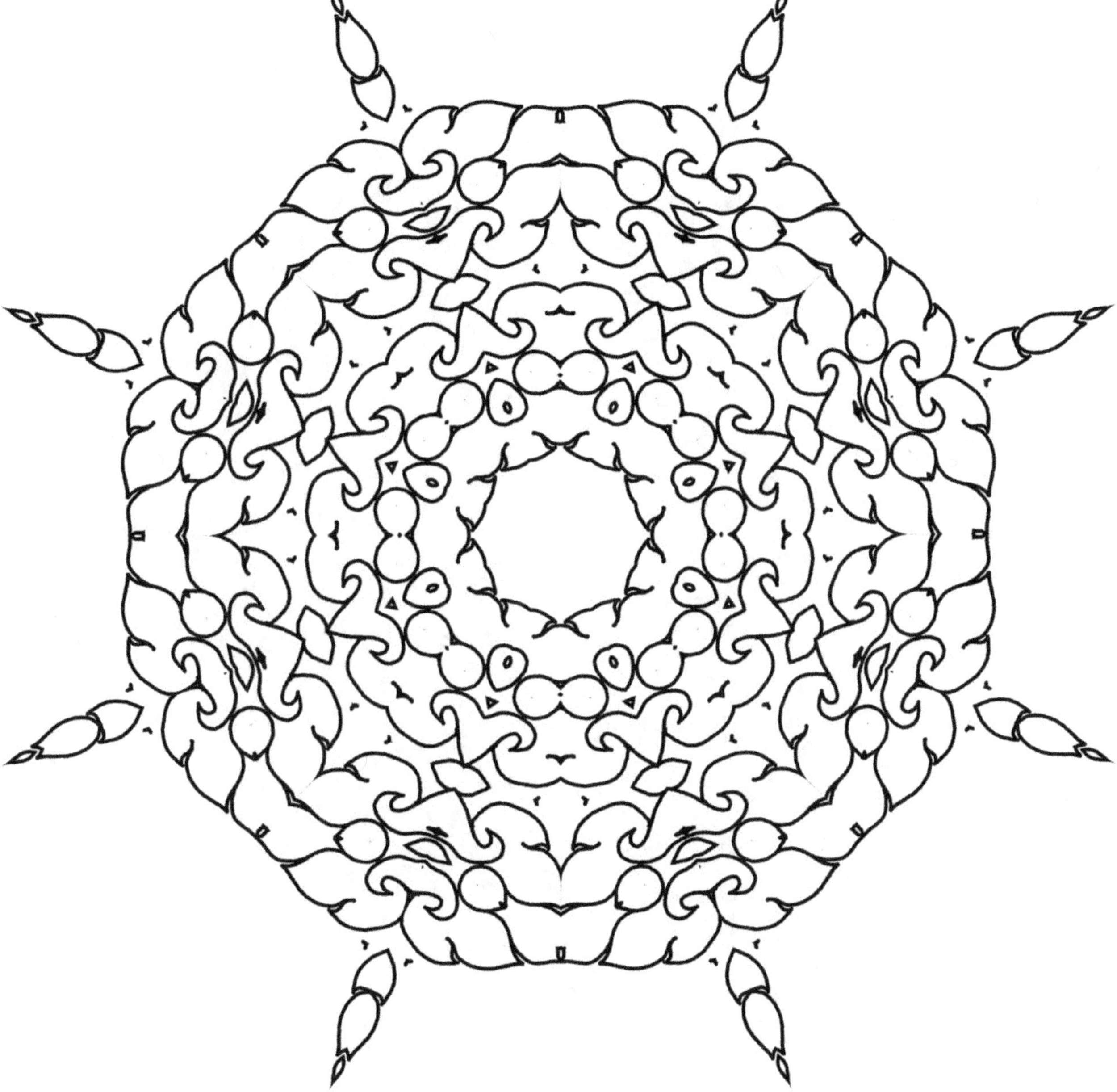

Thank you

www.ingramcontent.com/pod-product-compliance
Lightning Source LLC
Chambersburg PA
CBHW051946280526
45789CB00009B/3184